GOD'S PROMISES
FOR A
Mother's
HEART

...inspired by life

A Mother's Love

A mother is someone who dreams great dreams for you,
but then she lets you chase the dreams you have for yourself
and loves you just the same. In the end, she believes
in your dreams as much as you do.

A mother's love is something
that no one can explain,
It is made of deep devotion
and of sacrifice and pain....
It believes beyond believing
when the world around condemns,
And it glows with all the beauty
of the rarest, brightest gems.

HELEN STEINER RICE

Finally, all of you should be in agreement,
understanding each other, loving each other as family,
being kind and humble.

1 PETER 3:8 NCV

Women know
The way to rear up children (to be just);
They know a simple, merry, tender knack
Of tying sashes, fitting baby-shoes,
And stringing pretty words that make no sense,
And kissing full sense into empty words;
Which things are corals to cut life upon,
Although such trifles.

ELIZABETH BARRETT BROWNING

*If there be one thing pure...that can endure,
when all else passes away...it is a mother's love.*

MARCHIONESS DE SPADARA

Promises of the Day

Not every day of our lives is overflowing
with joy and celebration. But there are moments
when our hearts nearly burst within us for the sheer joy
of being alive. The first sight of our newborn babies,
the warmth of love in another's eyes, the fresh scent of rain
on a hot summer's eve—moments like these renew in us
a heartfelt appreciation for life.

GWEN ELLIS

Experience God in the breathless wonder and startling beauty
that is all around you. His sun shines warm upon your face.
His wind whispers in the treetops. Like the first rays
of morning light, celebrate the start of each day with God.

This is the day the LORD has made.
We will rejoice and be glad in it.

PSALM 118:24 NLT

Happy people...enjoy the fundamental,
often very simple things of life.... They savor the moment,
glad to be alive, enjoying their work, their families,
the good things around them. They are adaptable; they can bend
with the wind, adjust to the changes in their times,
enjoy the contest of life.... Their eyes are turned outward;
they are aware, compassionate. They have the capacity to love.

JANE CANFIELD

*We should look for reasons to celebrate—
an A on a paper—even a good hair day.*

PAM FARREL

Family Ties

We were a strange little band of characters, trudging through life
sharing diseases and toothpaste, coveting one another's desserts,
hiding shampoo, borrowing money, locking each other
out of our rooms, inflicting pain and kissing to heal it
in the same instant, loving, laughing, defending, and trying
to figure out the common thread that bound us all together.

ERMA BOMBECK

Just accept the fact that as long as you have
children in your home, your house is going to get messy.

LISA WHELCHEL

The family is a school of mutual help. Each member
depends on every other.... Each helps the other when
and where the help is most needed. And every word and deed
of unselfish love comes back in blessings on its author.

T. L. CUYLER

Having three children in three years was a great
pruning experience in my life. It was God's creative way of
putting me in a situation where I had to learn patience.

CYNTHIA HEALD

A family is a group of individuals who are related
to one another by marriage, birth, or adoption—
nothing more, nothing else. This is not merely human in origin.
It is God's marvelous creation.

JAMES DOBSON

Love each other with genuine affection, and take delight in honoring each other.

ROMANS 12:10 NLT

The Blessing of Gratitude

Gratitude unlocks the fullness of life. It turns what we have
into enough, and more.... It can turn a meal into a feast,
a house into a home, a stranger into a friend.
Gratitude makes sense of our past, brings peace for today,
and creates a vision for tomorrow.

MELODY BEATTIE

Feeling grateful or appreciative of someone or something
in your life actually attracts more of the things that you
appreciate and value into your life. And, the more of your life
that you like and appreciate, the healthier you'll be.

CHRISTIANE NORTHRUP

In ordinary life we hardly realize that we receive
a great deal more than we give, and that it is only
with gratitude that life becomes rich.

DIETRICH BONHOEFFER

Were there no God we would be in this glorious world
with grateful hearts and no one to thank.

CHRISTINA ROSSETTI

Be thankful. Let the word of Christ dwell in you richly
as you teach and admonish one another with all wisdom,
and as you sing psalms, hymns and spiritual songs
with gratitude in your hearts to God.

COLOSSIANS 3:15–16 NIV

Gratitude is the memory of the heart.

LYDIA MARIA CHILD

Love All Around

There is no need to plead that the love of God
shall fill our hearts as though He were unwilling to fill us....
Love is pressing around us on all sides like air.
Cease to resist it and instantly love takes possession.

AMY CARMICHAEL

Only He who created the wonders of the world
entwines hearts in an eternal way.

Love the Lord God with all your passion
and prayer and intelligence and energy.

MARK 12:30 MSG

Nothing can separate you from His love, absolutely nothing....
God is enough for time, and God is enough for eternity.
God is enough!

HANNAH WHITALL SMITH

God will never let you be shaken or moved
from your place near His heart.

JONI EARECKSON TADA

Open your hearts to the love God instills....
God loves you tenderly. What He gives you is not to be
kept under lock and key, but to be shared.

MOTHER TERESA

The human heart, at whatever age,
opens only to the heart that opens in return.

Maria Edgeworth

In God's Care

There will be days which are great and everything
goes as planned. There will be other days when we aren't sure
why we got out of bed. Regardless of which kind of day it is,
we can be assured that God takes care of our daily needs.

EMILIE BARNES

God is helping me to be content to set certain gifts on the shelf
at present for the sake of my family. He is teaching me that
He is more interested in what I am than in what I do.

SANDRA K. STRUBHAR

Be still, and in the quiet moments, listen to the voice
of your heavenly Father. His words can renew your spirit...
no one knows you and your needs like He does.

JANET L. SMITH

You are God's gift to each other for the living of these days.

RANDY BECTON

If you have a special need today, focus your full attention
on the goodness and greatness of your Father rather
than on the size of your need. Your need is so small
compared to His ability to meet it.

God...takes care of everyone in time of need.
His love never quits.

PSALM 136:23, 25 MSG

Blessed is the person who is too busy to worry in the daytime and too sleepy to worry at night.

The Strength of Family

Family faces are magic mirrors. Looking at people
who belong to us, we see the past, present, and future.

GAIL LUMET BUCKLEY

As if that weren't enough, you've blessed my family
so that it will continue in your presence always. Because you
have blessed it, God, it's really blessed—blessed for good!

1 CHRONICLES 17:16 MSG

Sooner or later we all discover that the important moments
in life are not the advertised ones, not the birthdays,
the graduations, the weddings, not the great goals achieved.
The real milestones are less prepossessing.
They come to the door of memory.

SUSAN B. ANTHONY

Call it clan, call it a network, call it a tribe, call it a family.
Whatever you call it, whoever you are, you need one.

JANE HOWARD

The effect of having other interests beyond
those domestic works well. The more one does and sees
and feels, the more one is able to do, and the more genuine
may be one's appreciation of fundamental things like home,
and love, and understanding companionship.

AMELIA EARHART

As for me and my family,
we will serve the LORD.

JOSHUA 24:15 NCV

Fresh Faith

To believe in God starts with a conclusion about Him,
develops into confidence in Him, and then matures
into a conversation with Him.

STUART BRISCOE

Faith is a living, daring confidence in God's grace, so sure
and certain that we could stake our lives on it a thousand times.

MARTIN LUTHER

Be assured, if you walk with Him and look to Him
and expect help from Him, He will never fail you.

GEORGE MUELLER

GOD's love, though, is ever and always, eternally present
to all who fear him, making everything right for them
and their children as they follow his Covenant ways.

PSALM 103:17–18 MSG

Know by the light of faith that God is present, and be content
with directing all your actions toward Him.

BROTHER LAWRENCE

God will never, never, never let us down if we have faith...
in Him. He will always look after us. So we must cleave to Jesus.
Our whole life must simply be woven into Jesus.

MOTHER TERESA

*Faith is the confidence that what we hope for will actually happen;
it gives us assurance about things we cannot see.*

HEBREWS 11:1 NLT

The Blessing of Dreams

It is necessary that we dream now and then.
No one ever achieved anything from the smallest to the greatest
unless the dream was dreamed first.

LAURA INGALLS WILDER

When you are inspired by a dream, God has hit the ball
into your court. Now you have to hit it back with commitment.

ROBERT SCHULLER

We need time to dream, time to remember,
and time to reach the infinite. Time to be.

GLADYS TABER

Now to him who is able to do immeasurably more
than all we ask or imagine, according to his power
that is at work within us, to him be glory.

EPHESIANS 3:20–21 NIV

How could I be anything but quite happy if I believed always
that all the past is forgiven, and all the present furnished
with power, and all the future bright with hope.

JAMES SMETHAM

Hope is not a dream, but a way
of making dreams become reality.

L. J. SUENENS

Do not pray for dreams equal to your powers.
Pray for powers equal to your dreams.

ADELAIDE ANN PROCTER

Thank You, Lord!

Let us continually offer the sacrifice of praise to God,
that is, the fruit of our lips, giving thanks to His name.
But do not forget to do good and to share,
for with such sacrifices God is well pleased.

HEBREWS 13:15–16 NKJV

Our thanksgiving today should include those things
which we take for granted, and we should continually
praise our God, who is true to His promise, who has
provided and retained the necessities for our living.

BETTY FUHRMAN

Thank God for dirty dishes;
They have a tale to tell.
While other folks go hungry,
We're eating pretty well.
With home, and health, and happiness,
We shouldn't want to fuss;
For by this stack of evidence,
God's very good to us.

Thanksgiving puts power in living, because it opens
the generators of the heart to respond gratefully,
to receive joyfully, and to react creatively.

God, of Your goodness give me Yourself, for You
are enough for me. And only in You do I have everything.

JULIAN OF NORWICH

*Thank You, Father, for loving all the little children of the world—
no matter how old we are.*

One of a Kind

Everyone has a unique role to fill in the world
and is important in some respect. Everyone, including
and perhaps especially you, is indispensable.

NATHANIEL HAWTHORNE

Though two children have the same parents, the same values,
the same everything, they turn out different.
Isn't that the genius of God?

You have a unique message to deliver, a unique song to sing,
a unique act of love to bestow. This message, this song,
and this act of love have been entrusted exclusively
to the one and only you.

JOHN POWELL

God loves us for ourselves. He values our love more
than He values galaxies of new created worlds.

A. W. TOZER

Heavenly Father, thank You for the unique personalities
that You have given to each and every child. Help me
to discover each talent and gift with which You have blessed
my children, and may I learn how to best cultivate each
of the blossoms You have planted within their souls. Amen.

KIM BOYCE

In his grace, God has given us different gifts
for doing certain things well.

ROMANS 12:6 NLT

*The value of a person is not measured on an applause meter;
it is measured in the heart and mind of God.*

JOHN FISHER

Taking Time to Love

Dear Lord, please help me to remember to take the time
to bestow the kisses today that I want loved ones
to remember tomorrow.

JENNIFER THOMAS

Make the most of every opportunity. Be gracious in your speech.
The goal is to bring out the best in others.

COLOSSIANS 4:5 MSG

Mama's order was heavenly. It had to do with thoroughness...
and taking plenty of time. It had to do with taking
plenty of time with me.

SUSANNAH LESSARD

Getting things accomplished isn't nearly as important
as taking time for love.

JANETTE OKE

Take time to notice all the usually unnoticed,
simple things in life. Delight in the never-ending hope
that's available every day!

WENDY MOORE

Live each day the fullest you can, not guaranteeing
there'll be a tomorrow, not dwelling endlessly on yesterday.

JANE SEYMOUR

Time is a very precious gift of God;
so precious that it's only given to us moment by moment.

AMELIA BARR

A Guiding Hand

I'll show my children right from wrong,
encourage dreams and hope;
explain respect for others,
while teaching them to cope
with outside pressures, inside fears,
a world that's less than whole;
and through it all I'll nurture
my children's most precious soul!
Though oftentimes a struggle,
this job I'll never trade;
for in my hand tomorrow lives...
a future God has made.

Teach your children why you believe what you believe.
Don't ask them to accept your beliefs blindly.
Don't be afraid to teach them to think for themselves.
God's Word can withstand the test.

PAUL MEIER

The God who made your children will hear your petitions.
He has promised to do so. After all, He loves them
more than you do.

JAMES DOBSON

Children, come and listen to me.
I will teach you to worship the LORD.

PSALM 34:11 NCV

Usually parents who are lucky in the kind of children they have, have children who are lucky in the kind of parents they have.

A Sense of Wonder

Whether sixty or sixteen, there is in every human being's heart
the love of wonder, the sweet amazement at the stars
and starlike things, the undaunted challenge of events,
the unfailing childlike appetite for what-next,
and the joy of the game of living.

SAMUEL ULLMAN

Many, O LORD my God,
are the wonders you have done.
The things you planned for us
no one can recount to you;
were I to speak and tell of them,
they would be too many to declare.

PSALM 40:5 NIV

Dear Lord, grant me the grace of wonder. Surprise me,
amaze me, awe me in every crevice of Your universe....
Each day enrapture me with Your marvelous things
without number. I do not ask to see the reason for it all;
I ask only to share the wonder of it all.

ABRAHAM JOSHUA HESCHEL

We need to recapture the power of imagination; we shall find
that life can be full of wonder, mystery, beauty, and joy.

SIR HAROLD SPENCER JONES

*I will praise you, O LORD, with all my heart;
I will tell of all your wonders.*

PSALM 9:1 NIV

A Covering of Prayer

I said a prayer for you today
And I know God must have heard,
I felt the answer in my heart
Although He spoke no word.
I asked that He'd be near you
At the start of each new day,
To grant you health and blessings
And friends to share the way.
I asked for happiness for you
In all things great and small,
But it was His loving care
I prayed for most of all.

Lord, thank You for my children. Please inspire me
with ways to show them my love and Yours.
I want them to feel appreciated. I want to help and
encourage them.... I want to bless them.

Quin Sherrer

When you were small
And just a touch away,
I covered you with blankets
Against the cool night air.
But now that you are tall
And out of reach,
I fold my hands
And cover you with prayer.

Dona Maddux Cooper

*I have not stopped giving thanks for you,
remembering you in my prayers.*

EPHESIANS 1:16 NIV

Living for Today

Lord...give me the gift of faith to be renewed and shared
with others each day. Teach me to live this moment only,
looking neither to the past with regret, nor the future
with apprehension. Let love be my aim and my life a prayer.

ROSEANN ALEXANDER-ISHAM

Live for today but hold your hands open to tomorrow.
Anticipate the future and its changes with joy.
There is a seed of God's love in every event,
every circumstance, every...situation
in which you may find yourself.

BARBARA JOHNSON

One of the most tragic things I know about human nature
is that all of us tend to put off living. We are all dreaming
of some magical rose garden over the horizon—
instead of enjoying the roses
that are blooming outside our windows today.

DALE CARNEGIE

Forgetting the past and looking forward to what lies ahead,
I press on to reach the end of the race and receive the heavenly
prize for which God, through Christ Jesus, is calling us.

PHILIPPIANS 3:13–14 NLT

Happy is the person who knows what to remember of the past, what to enjoy in the present, and what to plan for the future.

ARNOLD H. GLASGOW

The Lord Is My Strength

God's love is like a river springing up in the Divine Substance
and flowing endlessly through His creation, filling all things
with life and goodness and strength.

THOMAS MERTON

The LORD is my strength and my shield;
my heart trusts in him, and I am helped.
My heart leaps for joy and I will
give thanks to him in song.

PSALM 28:7 NIV

God never abandons anyone on whom He has set His love;
nor does Christ, the good shepherd, ever lose track
of His sheep.... We need to "wait upon the Lord"
in meditations on His majesty, till we find our strength
renewed through the writing of these things upon our hearts.

J. I. PACKER

Should we feel at times disheartened and discouraged,
a simple movement of heart toward God will renew our powers.
Whatever He may demand of us, He will give us at the moment
the strength and courage that we need.

FRANÇOIS FÉNELON

You have no strength but what God gives and you can have all the strength that God can give.

ANDREW MURRAY

The Blessing of Friendship

To have someone who wants to absorb us,
who wants to understand the shape and structure of our lives,
who will listen for more than our words,
is one of friendship's greatest gifts.

PAUL D. ROBBINS

Good communication is stimulating as black coffee,
and just as hard to sleep after.

ANNE MORROW LINDBERGH

Many women...have buoyed me up in times
of weariness and stress. Each friend was important....
Their words have seasoned my life. Influence, just like salt
shaken out, is hard to see, but its flavor is hard to miss.

PAM FARREL

Friendship is the fruit gathered from the trees
planted in the rich soil of love, and nurtured
with tender care and understanding.

ALMA L. WEIXELBAUM

Friendship is like love at its best: not blind
but sympathetically all-seeing; a support
which does not wait for understanding; an act of faith
which does not need, but always has, reason.

LOUIS UNTERMEYER

A friend loves at all times, and a brother is born for adversity.

PROVERBS 17:17 NIV

My Heart Is Content

I am still determined to be cheerful and happy,
in whatever situation I may be; for I have also learned
from experience that the greater part of our happiness
or misery depends upon our dispositions,
and not upon our circumstances.

MARTHA WASHINGTON

When we put people before possessions in our hearts,
we are sowing seeds of enduring satisfaction.

BEVERLY LAHAYE

God bless you and utterly satisfy your heart...with Himself.

AMY CARMICHAEL

My heart is content with just knowing
The treasures of life's little things;
The thrill of a child when it's snowing,
The trill of a bird in the spring.
My heart is content with just knowing
Fulfillment that true friendship brings;
It fills to the brim, overflowing
With pleasure in life's "little things."

JUNE MASTERS BACHER

If you're content to simply be yourself,
your life will count for plenty.

MATTHEW 23:11 MSG

Love, consolation and peace bloom only in the
garden of sweet contentment.

MARTHA ANDERSON

Praise and Adoration

It's who you are and the way you live that count before God.
Your worship must engage your spirit in the pursuit of truth.
That's the kind of people the Father is out looking for:
those who are simply and honestly themselves before him
in their worship. God is sheer being itself—Spirit.
Those who worship him must do it out of their very being,
their spirits, their true selves, in adoration.

JOHN 4:23–24 MSG

We can go through all the activities of our days in joyful
awareness of God's presence with whispered prayers of praise
and adoration flowing continuously from our hearts.

RICHARD J. FOSTER

It is right and good that we, for all things, at all times,
and in all places, give thanks and praise to You, O God.
We worship You, we confess to You, we praise You,
we bless You, we sing to You, and we give thanks to You:
Maker, Nourisher, Guardian, Healer, Lord, and Father of all.

LANCELOT ANDREWES

Walk and talk and work and laugh with your friends,
but behind the scenes, keep up the life of simple prayer
and inward worship.

THOMAS R. KELLY

*Love wholeheartedly, be surprised, give thanks and praise—
then you will discover the fullness of your life.*

DAVID STEINDL-RAST

Living in Truth

Open my eyes that I may see
Glimpses of truth Thou hast for me.
Place in my hands the wonderful key
That shall unclasp and set me free:
Silently now I wait for Thee,
Ready, my God, Thy will to see;
Open my eyes, illumine me,
Spirit divine!

CLARA H. FISKE SCOTT

Living the truth in your heart without compromise
brings kindness into the world.

EIGHTEENTH CENTURY MONK

To follow truth as blind men long for light,
To do my best from dawn of day till night,
To keep my heart fit for His holy sight,
And answer when He calls.
This is my task.

MAUDE LOUISE RAY

I am amazed by the sayings of Christ.
They seem truer than anything I have ever read.
And they certainly turn the world upside down.

KATHERINE BUTLER HATHAWAY

*Jesus answered, "I am the way and the truth and the life.
No one comes to the Father except through me."*

JOHN 14:6 NIV

Blessings for the Children

There is no greater pleasure than bringing to the uncluttered,
supple mind of a child the delight of knowing God
and the many rich things He has given us to enjoy.

GLADYS M. HUNT

It's not what you think that influences your child;
it's what you communicate.

CHARLES STANLEY

The time needed to talk to a child, time given to an impulse—
only you can measure the value. For whatever ways
you spend your time, it ought to pay high dividends
in meeting physical needs and enriching
the mind and spirit of each family member.

ALICE FULTON SKELSEY

We will not hide these truths from our children;
we will tell the next generation
about the glorious deeds of the LORD,
about his power and his mighty wonders.

PSALM 78:4 NLT

What parent can tell when some fragmentary gift
of knowledge or wisdom will enrich her children's lives?

HELENA RUBINSTEIN

Recognizing the good in children is one of the greatest gifts we can give to them.

Time to Enjoy

Slow down and enjoy life. It's not only the scenery you miss
by going too fast—you also miss the sense
of where you are going and why.

EDDIE CANTOR

Half the joy of life is in little things taken on the run.
Let us run if we must—even the sands do that—but let us
keep our hearts young and our eyes open that nothing
worth our while shall escape us. And everything is worth
its while if we only grasp it and its significance.

VICTOR CHERBULIEZ

Dear friend, I pray that you may enjoy good health and that all
may go well with you, even as your soul is getting along well.

3 JOHN 1:2 NIV

Where does the time go, Lord? I can't seem
to get everything done in one day. Maybe I am trying to do
too many things. No matter how busy it gets,
help me to spend time with You every single day.
If I don't, slow me down so I can. Thank You, Lord.

MARILYN JANSEN

When you have laboriously accomplished your daily task,
go to sleep in peace. God is awake.

VICTOR HUGO

God has made everything beautiful for its own time.
He has planted eternity in the human heart.

ECCLESIASTES 3:11 NLT

Light for the Way

A new path lies before us;
We're not sure where it leads;
But God goes on before us,
Providing all our needs.
This path, so new, so different
Exciting as we climb,
Will guide us in His perfect will
Until the end of time.

LINDA MAURICE

I believe that God is in me as the sun is in the color
and fragrance of a flower—the Light in my darkness,
the Voice in my silence.

HELEN KELLER

God has not promised skies always blue,
flower-strewn pathways all our lives through;
God has not promised sun without rain,
joy without sorrow, peace without pain.
But God has promised strength for the day,
rest for the labor, light for the way,
grace for the trials, help from above,
unfailing sympathy, undying love.

ANNIE JOHNSON FLINT

Your word is a lamp to my feet and a light for my path.

PSALM 119:105 NIV

*Faith in small things has repercussions that ripple all the way out.
In a huge, dark room a little match can light up the place.*

JONI EARECKSON TADA

At Mother's Knee

Whether we are poets or parents or teachers
or artists or gardeners, we must start where we are
and use what we have. In the process of creation
and relationship, what seems mundane and trivial
may show itself to be holy, precious, part of a pattern.

LUCI SHAW

To discipline a child produces wisdom....
Discipline your children, and they will give you peace of mind
and will make your heart glad.

PROVERBS 29:15, 17 NLT

God, help me to be honest
so my children will learn honesty.
Help me to be kind
so my children will learn kindness.
Help me to be faithful
so my children will learn faith.
Help me to love
so that my children will be loving.

MARIAN WRIGHT EDELMAN

The most important thing she'd learned over the years
was that there was no way to be a perfect mother
and a million ways to be a good one.

JILL CHURCHILL

*Train up a child in the way he should go,
and when he is old he will not depart from it.*

PROVERBS 22:6 NKJV

Little Acts of Kindness

Kindness is the only service that will stand the
storms of life and not wash out. It will wear well
and be remembered long after the prism of politeness
or the complexion of courtesy has faded away.

Notice words of compassion. Seek out deeds of kindness.
These are like the doves from heaven, pointing out to you
who are the ones blessed with inner grace and beauty.

CHRISTOPHER DE VINCK

The greatest thing a person can do for their heavenly Father
is to be kind to some of His other children....
How easily it is done. How instantaneously it acts.
How infallibly it is remembered.

HENRY DRUMMOND

If you can help anybody even a little, be glad;
up the steps of usefulness and kindness,
God will lead you on to happiness and friendship.

MALTBIE D. BABCOCK

The older you get the more you realize that kindness
is synonymous with happiness.

LIONEL BARRYMORE

*Be kind to one another, tenderhearted,
forgiving one another, even as God in Christ forgave you.*

EPHESIANS 4:32 NKJV

The Gift of Simplicity

Don't ever let yourself get so busy that you miss those
little but important extras in life—the beauty of a day...
the smile of a friend...the serenity of a quiet moment alone.
For it is often life's smallest pleasures and gentlest joys
that make the biggest and most lasting difference.

It doesn't take monumental feats to make the world
a better place. It can be as simple as letting someone
go ahead of you in a grocery line.

BARBARA JOHNSON

Let us consider how we may spur one another on
toward love and good deeds.

HEBREWS 10:24 NIV

Simplicity will enable you to leap lightly.
Increasingly you will find yourself living in a state of grace,
finding...the sacred in the ordinary,
the mystical in the mundane.

DAVID YOUNT

A devout life does bring wealth, but it's the rich simplicity
of being yourself before God. Since we entered the world
penniless and will leave it penniless, if we have
bread on the table and shoes on our feet, that's enough.

1 TIMOTHY 6:6–8 MSG

*It isn't the great big pleasures that count the most;
it's making a great deal out of the little ones.*

Taking Care of Mom

Though motherhood is the most important
of all the professions—requiring more knowledge
than any other department in human affairs—there was no
attention given to preparation for this office.

ELIZABETH CADY STANTON

As a mother, my job is to take care of what is possible
and trust God with the impossible.

RUTH BELL GRAHAM

Part of the curse of motherhood is never knowing
if you're doing a good job. But part of the joy
is realizing no one's really keeping score.

DALE HANSON BOURKE

Motherhood is...the biggest on-the-job
training program in existence today.

ERMA BOMBECK

More so than any other human relationship, in fact,
overwhelmingly more, motherhood means being instantly
interruptible, responsive, and responsible.

Mother had a thousand thoughts to get through within a day,
and...most of these were about avoiding disaster.

NATALIE KUSZ

*Cast your cares on the Lord
and he will sustain you.*

PSALM 55:22 NIV

Close to Him

Incredible as it may seem, God wants our companionship.
He wants to have us close to Him. He wants to be a father to us,
to shield us, to protect us, to counsel us,
and to guide us in our way through life.

BILLY GRAHAM

God still draws near to us in the ordinary, commonplace,
everyday experiences and places.... He comes in surprising ways.

HENRY GARIEPY

It is when things go wrong, when good things
do not happen, when our prayers seem to have been lost,
that God is most present.

MADELEINE L'ENGLE

The sunshine dancing on the water, the lulling sound of waves
rolling into the shore, the glittering stars against the night sky—
all God's light, His warmth, His majesty—our Father of light
reaching out to us, drawing each of us closer to Himself.

WENDY MOORE

By putting the gift of yearning for God into every human
being's heart, God at the same time draws all people made in
God's image to God's self and into their own true selves.

ROBERTA BONDI

*Draw near to God
and He will draw near to you.*

JAMES 4:8 NKJV

A Generous Spirit

Love in the heart wasn't put there to stay;
love isn't love 'til you give it away.

OSCAR HAMMERSTEIN II

If your gift is to encourage others, be encouraging.
If it is giving, give generously.... Don't just pretend
to love other. Really love them.

ROMANS 12:8–9 NLT

Don't just get older, get better. Live realistically.
Give generously. Adapt willingly. Trust fearlessly. Rejoice daily.

CHARLES SWINDOLL

Giving is the secret of a healthy life...
not necessarily money, but whatever one has
of encouragement and sympathy and understanding.

JOHN D. ROCKEFELLER JR.

Love is not the saying of the words but the giving of the self.

ROBERT LANDER

Love is not getting, but giving.... It is goodness and honor
and peace and pure living—yes, love is that and it is
the best thing in the world and the thing that lives the longest.

HENRY VAN DYKE

*Be happy with what you have and are,
be generous with both, and you won't have to hunt for happiness.*

WILLIAM E. GLADSTONE

My Mother, My Friend

Having someone who understands is a great blessing
for ourselves. Being someone who understands
is a great blessing to others.

JANETTE OKE

Oh, the comfort, the inexpressible comfort of feeling safe
with a person—having neither to weigh thoughts nor
measure words, but pouring them all right out just as they are,
chaff and grain together, certain that a faithful hand will take
and sift them, keep what is worth keeping and then,
with the breath of kindness, blow the rest away.

DINAH MARIA MULOCK CRAIK

Instant availability without continuous presence
is probably the best role a mother can play.

L. BAILYN

Make me very happy by having the same thoughts,
sharing the same love, and having one mind and purpose.

PHILIPPIANS 2:2 NCV

Listening...means taking a vigorous, human interest in what is
being told us. You can listen like a blank wall or like a splendid
auditorium where every sound comes back fuller and richer.

ALICE DUER MILLER

*We should all have one person who knows
how to bless us despite the evidence.*

PHYLLIS THEROUX

A Beautiful Life

Consider the lilies, how they grow: they neither toil nor spin;
and yet I say to you, even Solomon in all his glory was not
arrayed like one of these. If then God so clothes the grass,
which today is in the field and tomorrow is thrown
into the oven, how much more will He clothe you?

LUKE 12:27–28 NKJV

Something deep in all of us yearns for God's beauty,
and we can find it no matter where we are.

SUE MONK KIDD

Beauty puts a face on God. When we gaze at nature,
at a loved one, at a work of art, our soul immediately recognizes
and is drawn to the face of God.

MARGARET BROWNLEY

Every time you smile at someone, it is an action of love,
a gift to that person, a beautiful thing.

MOTHER TERESA

The Lord is all I need. He takes care of me. My share in life
has been pleasant; my part has been beautiful.

PSALM 16:5–6 NCV

Isn't it a wonderful morning? The world looks like something
God had just imagined for His own pleasure.

LUCY MAUD MONTGOMERY

*You are God's created beauty and the focus
of His affection and delight.*

JANET L. SMITH

Providing All Our Needs

I must simply be thankful, and I am,
for all the Lord has provided for me, whether
big or small in the eyes of someone else.

MABEL P. ADAMSON

You can trust God right now to supply all your needs for today.
And if your needs are more tomorrow, His supply
will be greater also.

Throughout the Bible, when God asked someone
to do something, methods, means, materials
and specific directions were always provided.
That person had one thing to do: obey.

ELISABETH ELLIOT

Those who know God as their Father know the whole secret.
They are His heirs, and may enter now into possession
of all that is necessary for their present needs.

HANNAH WHITALL SMITH

You care for the land and water it;
you enrich it abundantly.
The streams of God are filled with water
to provide the people with grain,
for so you have ordained it.

PSALM 65:9 NIV

God's gifts make us truly wealthy.
His loving supply never shall leave us wanting.

BECKY LAIRD

Childhood Memories

There is nothing higher and stronger and more wholesome
and useful for life in later years than some good memory,
especially a memory connected with childhood, with home.

FYODOR DOSTOYEVSKY

There was a place in childhood that I remember well,
And there a voice of sweetest tone bright fairy tales did tell.

SAMUEL LOVER

O Lord, you alone are my hope
I've trusted you, O LORD, from childhood.
Yes, you have been with me from birth;
from my mother's womb you have cared for me.
No wonder I am always praising you!

PSALM 71:5–6 NLT

A family is a "gallery of memories" to those who have been
blessed by the presence of children.

JAMES DOBSON

Take the gift of this moment and make something
beautiful of it. Few worthwhile experiences just happen,
memories are made on purpose.

GLORIA GAITHER

How dear to the heart are the scenes of my childhood,
when fond recollection presents them to view.

SAMUEL WOODWORTH

Memory is the treasury and guardian of all things.

CICERO

Enjoying His Presence

The Lord's chief desire is to reveal Himself to you and,
in order for Him to do that, He gives you abundant grace.
The Lord gives you the experience of enjoying His presence.
He touches you, and His touch is so delightful that,
more than ever, you are drawn inwardly to Him.

MADAME JEANNE GUYON

You're all I want in heaven! You're all I want on earth....
I'm in the very presence of GOD—
oh, how refreshing it is! I've made Lord GOD my home.
GOD, I'm telling the world what you do!

PSALM 73:25, 28 MSG

Let God have you, and let God love you—
and don't be surprised if your heart begins to hear music
you've never heard and your feet learn to dance as never before.

MAX LUCADO

O the pure delight of a single hour
that before Thy throne I spend,
When I kneel in prayer, and with Thee, my God,
I commune as friend with friend!

FANNY J. CROSBY

Life need not be easy to be joyful. Joy is not
the absence of trouble, but the presence of Christ.

WILLIAM VANDERHOVEN

*Let the godly rejoice. Let them be glad in God's presence.
Let them be filled with joy.*

PSALM 68:3 NLT

The Beauty of Motherhood

Most of all the other beautiful things in life come
by twos and threes, by dozens and hundreds.
Plenty of roses, stars, sunsets, rainbows, brothers and sisters,
aunts and cousins, comrades and friends—
but only one mother in the whole world.

KATE DOUGLAS WIGGIN

Ask any four-year-old boy, "Who's the most beautiful
woman in the world?" His mommy! Ask any grown daughter
caring for her aging mother the same question,
and you'll get the same answer.... Moms spend a lifetime
humbling themselves in taking care of others.
Nothing is more attractive.

LISA WHELCHEL

Therefore, as God's chosen people, holy and dearly loved,
clothe yourselves with compassion, kindness, humility,
gentleness and patience.

COLOSSIANS 3:12 NIV

As God's workmanship, we deserve to be treated,
and to treat ourselves, with affection and affirmation,
regardless of our appearance or performance.

MARY ANN MAYO

To be a child is to know the joy of living.
To have a child is to know the beauty of life.

The Wonder of Wisdom

For the wisdom of the wisest being God has made
ends in wonder; and there is nothing on earth so wonderful
as the budding soul of a little child.

LUCY LARCOM

What a wildly wonderful world, GOD! You made it all,
with Wisdom at your side, made earth overflow
with your wonderful creations.

PSALM 104:24 MSG

I am convinced beyond a shadow of any doubt that the most
valuable pursuit we can embark upon is to know God.

KAY ARTHUR

All things bright and beautiful,
All creatures great and small,
All things wise and wonderful,
The Lord God made them all.

CECIL FRANCES ALEXANDER

A wise gardener plants his seeds, then has the good sense not
to dig them up every few days to see if a crop is on the way.
Likewise, we must be patient as God brings the answers...
in His own good time.

QUIN SHERRER

A child's hand in yours—what tenderness and power it arouses.
You are instantly the very touchstone of wisdom and strength.

MARJORIE HOLMES

Homegrown Happiness

How necessary it is to cultivate a spirit of joy.
It is a psychological truth that the physical acts of reverence
and devotion make one feel devout. The courteous gesture
increases one's respect for others. To act lovingly is to
begin to feel loving, and certainly to act joyfully brings
joy to others which in turn makes one feel joyful.
I believe we are called to the duty of delight.

DOROTHY DAY

Sometimes the laughter in mothering
is the recognition of the ironies and absurdities.
Sometime, though, it's just pure, unthinking delight.

BARBARA SCHAPIRO

If children are to keep their inborn sense of wonder...
they need the companionship of at least one adult
who can share it, rediscovering with them the joy,
excitement, and mystery of the world we live in.

RACHEL CARSON

The Lord has filled my heart with joy; I feel very strong
in the Lord.... I am glad because you have helped me!

1 SAMUEL 2:1 NCV

Joy is the feeling of grinning on the inside.

MELBA COLGROVE

*To be able to find joy in another's joy,
that is the secret of happiness.*

Talking to God

We need quiet time to examine our lives openly and honestly....
Spending quiet time alone gives your mind an opportunity
to renew itself and create order.

Susan L. Taylor

If a care is too small to be turned into a prayer then it is
too small to be made into a burden.

Open wide the windows of our spirits and fill us full of light;
open wide the door of our hearts that we may receive
and entertain You with all the powers of our adoration.

Christina Rossetti

I find joy in receiving my children in prayer as gifts from God.
As I do it almost daily, I find that it enhances my appreciation
of them and my relationship with them.

Jack Taylor

Whate'er the care which breaks thy rest,
Whate'er the wish that swells thy breast;
Spread before God that wish, that care,
And change anxiety to prayer.

You pay God a compliment by asking great things of Him.

Teresa of Avila

Always be joyful. Pray continually, and give thanks whatever happens. That is what God wants for you in Christ Jesus.

1 THESSALONIANS 5:16–18 NCV

You Are Blessed with Talent

Not everyone possesses boundless energy
or a conspicuous talent. We are not equally blessed
with great intellect or physical beauty or emotional strength.
But we have all been given the same ability to be faithful.

GIGI GRAHAM TCHIVIDJIAN

Do all the good you can
By all the means you can
In all the ways you can
In all the places you can
To all the people you can
As long as ever you can.

JOHN WESLEY

No one can arrive from being talented alone.
God gives talent, work transforms talent into genius.

ANNA PAVLOVA

Have a purpose in life, and having it, throw into your work
such strength of mind and muscle as God has given you.

THOMAS CARLYLE

Whatever you do, whether in word or deed,
do it all in the name of the Lord Jesus, giving thanks
to God the Father through him.

COLOSSIANS 3:17 NIV

If your lips can speak a word of encouragement to a weary soul,
you have a talent.

EVA J. CUMMINGS

The Simplicity of Childhood

"Unless you accept God's kingdom in the simplicity of a child,
you'll never get in." Then, gathering the children up in his arms,
[Jesus] laid his hands of blessing on them.

MARK 10:15–16 MSG

When you pray, do not try to express yourself in fancy words,
for often it is the simple repetitious phrases of a little child
that our Father in heaven finds most irresistible.

JOHN CLIMACUS

The wonder of our Lord is that He is so accessible to us
in the common things of our lives: the cup of water...
breaking of the bread...welcoming children into our arms...
fellowship over a meal...giving thanks.

NANCIE CARMICHAEL

A mother can see beauty
In the very smallest thing
For there's a little bit of heaven
In a small child's offering.

KATHERINE NELSON DAVIS

My childhood home was the home of a woman
with a genius for inventing daily life, who found happiness
in the simplest of gestures.

LAURA FRONTY

*With our children who thrive on simple pleasures,
our work and our entire society can be renewed.*

SARA WENGER SHENK

All Creation Sings

It is an extraordinary and beautiful thing
that God, in creation...works with the beauty of matter;
the reality of things; the discoveries of the senses,
all five of them; so that we, in turn, may hear
the grass growing; see a face springing to life
in love and laughter.... The offerings of creation...
our glimpses of truth.

MADELEINE L'ENGLE

It is always wise to stop wishing for things long enough
to enjoy the fragrance of those now flowering.

PATRICE GIFFORD

In all ranks of life the human heart yearns for the beautiful,
and the beautiful things that God makes are His gift to all alike.

HARRIET BEECHER STOWE

Every good action and every perfect gift is from God.
These good gifts come down from the Creator of the sun,
moon, and stars, who does not change
like their shifting shadows. God decided to give us life
through the word of truth so we might be
the most important of all the things he made.

JAMES 1:17–18 NCV

Loving Creator, help me reawaken my childlike sense
of wonder at the delights of Your world!

MARILYN MORGAN HELLEBERG

Promises in the Present

Normal day, let me be aware of the treasure you are.
Let me learn from you, love you, bless you before you depart.
Let me not pass you by in quest of some
rare and perfect tomorrow.

Women of adventure have conquered their fates
and know how to live exciting and fulfilling lives
right where they are. They have learned to reinvent themselves
and find creative ways to enjoy the world and their place in it.
They know how to take mini-vacations, stop and smell the roses,
and live fully in the moment.

BARBARA JENKINS

Children have neither past nor future;
they enjoy the present, which very few of us do.

JEAN DE LA BRUYÉRE

Let the day suffice, with all its joys and failings,
its little triumphs and defeats.... Happily, if sleepily,
welcome evening as a time of rest,
and let it slip away, losing nothing.

KATHLEEN NORRIS

I have learned the secret of being content in any
and every situation, whether well fed or hungry,
whether living in plenty or in want.

PHILIPPIANS 4:12 NIV

*If you surrender completely to the moments as they pass,
you live more richly those moments.*

ANNE MORROW LINDBERGH

The Truth in Love

Love never gives up.
Love cares more for others than for self.
Love doesn't want what it doesn't have.
Love doesn't strut...
Isn't always "me first,"
Doesn't fly off the handle,
Doesn't keep score of the sins of others...
Takes pleasure in the flowering of truth,
Puts up with anything,
Trusts God always,
Always looks for the best,
Never looks back,
But keeps going to the end.

1 CORINTHIANS 13:4–7 MSG

Love. No greater theme can be emphasized.
No stronger message can be proclaimed. No finer song
can be sung. No better truth can be imagined.

CHARLES SWINDOLL

I wish you peace—in the world in which you live
and in the smallest corner of the heart where truth is kept.
I wish you faith—to help define your living and your life.
More I cannot wish you—except perhaps love—
to make all the rest worthwhile.

ROBERT A. WARD

The deepest truth blooms only from the deepest love.

HEINRICH HEINE

His Promised Attention

See each morning a world made anew, as if it were
the morning of the very first day;...treasure and use it,
as if it were the final hour of the very last day.

FAY HARTZELL ARNOLD

This is the real gift: you have been given the breath of life,
designed with a unique, one-of-a-kind soul that exists forever—
the way that you choose to live it doesn't change the fact
that you've been given the gift of *being* now and forever.
Priceless in value, you are handcrafted by God,
who has a personal design and plan for each of us.

WENDY MOORE

The God who created, names, and numbers the stars
in the heavens also numbers the hairs of my head....
He pays attention to very big things and to very small ones.
What matters to me matters to Him, and that changes my life.

ELISABETH ELLIOT

Store up for yourselves treasures in heaven,
where moth and rust do not destroy, and where thieves
do not break in and steal. For where your treasure is,
there your heart will be also.

MATTHEW 6:20–21 NIV

*The greatest gift we can give one another
is rapt attention to one another's existence.*

SUE ATCHLEY EBAUGH

The Heritage of Children

Every material goal, even if it is met, will pass away.
But the heritage of children is timeless.
Our children are our messages to the future.

BILLY GRAHAM

I will sing of the mercies of the LORD forever;
With my mouth will I make known
Your faithfulness to all generations.

PSALM 89:1 NKJV

There is nothing quite so deeply satisfying as the solidarity
of a family united across the generations and miles
by a common faith and history.

SARA WENGER SHENK

Life is no brief candle to me. It is a...splendid torch...
and I want to make it burn as brightly as possible
before handing it over to future generations.

GEORGE BERNARD SHAW

Favorite people, favorite places,
favorite memories of the past...
These are the joys of a lifetime...
these are the things that last.

Father, help me to take the time to create stories with my
children. May good memories hold the generations together.

SCOTT WALKER

We live in the present, we dream of the future,
but we learn eternal truths from the past.

LUCY MAUD MONTGOMERY

God Our Father

Blessed be the God and Father of our Lord Jesus Christ,
the Father of mercies and God of all comfort,
who comforts us in all our tribulation, that we may be able
to comfort those who are in any trouble, with the comfort
with which we ourselves are comforted by God.

2 CORINTHIANS 1:3–4 NKJV

As a rose fills a room with its fragrance,
so will God's love fill our lives.

MARGARET BROWNLEY

God is every moment totally aware of each one of us.
Totally aware in intense concentration and love....
No one passes through any area of life, happy or tragic,
without the attention of God.

EUGENIA PRICE

Before anything else, above all else, beyond everything else,
God loves us. God loves us extravagantly, ridiculously,
without limit or condition. God is in love with us....
God yearns for us.

ROBERTA BONDI

Whoever walks toward God one step,
God runs toward him two.

JEWISH PROVERB

*The treasure our heart searches for
is found in the ocean of God's love.*

JANET L. SMITH

Promised Dividends

Choices can change our lives profoundly. The choice to mend
a broken relationship, to say yes to a difficult assignment,
to lay aside some important work to play with a child,
to visit some forgotten person—
these small choices may affect our lives eternally.

GLORIA GAITHER

Let your light shine before men, that they may see
your good deeds and praise your Father in heaven.

MATTHEW 5:16 NIV

Can you measure the worth of a sunbeam,
The worth of a treasured smile,
The value of love and of giving,
The things that make life worthwhile?...
Can you measure the value of friendship,
Of knowing that someone is there,
Of faith and of hope and of courage,
A treasured and goodly share?

GARNETT ANN SCHULTZ

We must not, in trying to think about how we can
make a big difference, ignore the small daily differences
we can make which, over time, add up to big differences
that we often cannot foresee.

MARIAN WRIGHT EDELMAN

Invest in people rather than things
for herein lies eternal dividends.

A Blessed Influence

What we feel, think, and do this moment influences both our
present and the future in ways we may never know. Begin.
Start right where you are. Consider your possibilities
and find inspiration...to add more meaning and zest to your life.

ALEXANDRA STODDARD

The blossom cannot tell what becomes of its fragrance
as it drifts away, just as no person can tell what becomes
of her influence as she continues through life.

The fullness of our heart is expressed in our eyes, in our touch,
in what we write, in what we say, in the way we walk,
the way we receive, the way we need.

MOTHER TERESA

How blessed the man you train, GOD,
the woman you instruct in your Word,
providing a circle of quiet
within the clamor of evil....
God will never walk away from his people,
never desert his precious people.
Rest assured that justice is on its way
and every good heart put right.

PSALM 94:12–15 MSG

A mother is not a person to lean on,
but a person to make leaning unnecessary.

DOROTHY CANFIELD FISHER

*There is no influence so powerful
as that of the mother.*

SARAH JOSEPHA HALE

Wonderful Peace

We give thanks for the darkness of the night where lies
the world of dreams.... Give us good dreams and memory
of them so that we may carry their poetry and mystery
into our daily lives.... Let us restore the night and reclaim it
as a sanctuary of peace, where silence shall be music to our hearts
and darkness shall throw light upon our souls.

MICHAEL LEUNIG

O heavenly Father, protect and bless all things that have breath:
guard them from all evil and let them sleep in peace.

ALBERT SCHWEITZER

Only God gives true peace—a quiet gift He sets within us
just when we think we've exhausted our search for it.

May God kiss you with His peace, as a mother
kisses her little child. And may you know that peace isn't
a pot of gold rewarded to you after chasing
some rainbow's end—it's a gift.

May your footsteps set you upon a lifetime journey of love.
May you wake each day with His blessings
and sleep each night in His keeping.
And may you always walk in His tender care.

*Grace and peace to you from God our Father
and from the Lord Jesus Christ.*

ROMANS 1:7 NIV

God Bless Your Children

I wish I had a box,
the biggest I could find,
I'd fill it right up to the brim
with everything that's kind.
A box without a lock, of course,
and never any key;
for everything inside that box
would then be offered free.
Grateful words for joys received
I'd freely give away.
Oh, let us open wide a box
of praise for every day.

Each day is a treasure box of gifts from God,
just waiting to be opened. Open your gifts with excitement.
You will find forgiveness attached to ribbons of joy.
You will find love wrapped in sparkling gems.

JOAN CLAYTON

Just as Jesus took the children, put His hands on them
and blessed them...we can hold our children in our arms,
touching, blessing, and praying over them.

QUIN SHERRER

Bless our children, God, and help us so to fashion their souls
by precept and example that they may ever love the good,
flee from sin, revere Your Word, and honor Your name.

UNION PRAYER BOOK

*May the LORD richly bless both
you and your children.*

PSALM 115:14 NLT

Inspiration to Love

Look deep within yourself and recognize what brings
life and grace into your heart. It is this that can be shared
with those around you. You are loved by God.
This is an inspiration to love.

CHRISTOPHER DE VINCK

My God, I give You this day.
I offer You, now all of the good that I shall do
And I promise to accept, for love of You,
All of the difficulty that I shall meet.
Help me to conduct myself during this day
In a manner pleasing to You.
Amen.

FRANCIS DE SALES

To be grateful is to recognize the Love of God
in everything He has given us—and He has given us everything.
Every breath we draw is a gift of His love, every moment
of existence is a gift of grace.

THOMAS MERTON

Your unfailing love, O LORD, is as vast as the heavens;
your faithfulness reaches beyond the clouds.
Your righteousness is like the mighty mountains,
your justice like the ocean depths....
How precious is your unfailing love, O God!

PSALM 36:5–7 NLT

The love of the Father is like a sudden rain shower that will pour forth when you least expect it, catching you up into wonder and praise.

Wisdom to Live By

At the end of your life you will never regret
not having passed one more test, not winning one more verdict,
or not closing one more deal. You will regret time not spent
with a husband, a friend, a child, or a parent.

BARBARA BUSH

Whenever I need help being a mother, I remember
my mother and grandmother, women who planted seeds
of wisdom in my soul, like a secret garden,
to flower even in the bitterest cold.

JUDITH TOWSE-ROBERTS

Heavenly Father, please give me wisdom in daily
protecting my children. Whether it's concerning the people
they come in contact with, the television and videos they watch,
or the many other issues that affect them, may I be aware
of my responsibility to guide and nurture their minds. Amen.

KIM BOYCE

We ought to be able to learn things secondhand.
There is not enough time for us
to make all the mistakes ourselves.

HARRIET HALL

Teach us to number our days aright,
that we may gain a heart of wisdom.

PSALM 90:12 NIV

The wise don't expect to find life worth living;
they make it that way.

The Promise of Faith

If it can be verified, we don't need faith.... Faith is
for that which lies on the other side of reason. Faith is what
makes life bearable, with all its tragedies and ambiguities
and sudden, startling joys.

MADELEINE L'ENGLE

I pray that Christ will live in your hearts by faith and that
your life will be strong in love and be built on love.

EPHESIANS 3:17 NCV

True faith drops its letter in the post office box and lets it go.
Distrust holds on to a corner of it and wonders
that the answer never comes.

L. B. COWMAN

Finding acceptance with joy, whatever the circumstances of
life—whether they are petty annoyances or fiery trials—
this is a living faith that grows.

MARY LOU STEIGLEDER

Faith means being sure of what we hope for...now.
It means knowing something is real, this moment,
all around you, even when you don't see it. Great faith isn't
the ability to believe long and far into the misty future.
It's simply taking God at His word and taking the next step.

JONI EARECKSON TADA

*Faith expects from God
what is beyond all expectations.*

Irreplaceable

If God gives such attention to the appearance of wildflowers—
most of which are never even seen—don't you think he'll
attend to you, take pride in you, do his best for you?

What I'm trying to do here is to get you to relax, to not be so
preoccupied with *getting*, so you can respond to God's *giving*.
People who don't know God and the way he works fuss over
these things, but you know both God and how he works.

Steep your life in God-reality, God-initiative, God-provisions.
Don't worry about missing out. You'll find all your everyday
human concerns will be met.

MATTHEW 6:30–33 MSG

All that we have and are is one of the unique
and never-to-be repeated ways God has chosen to express
Himself in space and time. Each of us, made in His image
and likeness, is yet another promise He has made to the universe
that He will continue to love it and care for it.

BRENNAN MANNING

We have missed the full impact of the Gospel if we have not
discovered what it is to be ourselves, loved by God,
irreplaceable in His sight, unique among our fellow men.

BRUCE LARSON

*Embrace your uniqueness. Time is much too short
to be living someone else's life.*

KOBI YAMADA

Through the Eyes of a Child

My child took a crayon
In her little hand
And started to draw
As if by command.

I looked on with pleasure
But couldn't foresee
What the few simple lines
Were going to be.

What are you drawing?
I asked, by and by.
I'm making a picture
Of God in the sky.

But nobody knows
What God looks like, I sighed.
They will when I'm finished
She calmly replied.

SHERWIN KAUFMAN

Jesus said, "Let the little children come to me,
and do not hinder them, for the kingdom of heaven
belongs to such as these."

MATTHEW 19:14 NIV

The most successful parents are those who have the skill
to get behind the eyes of a child, seeing what they see,
thinking what they think, feeling what they feel.

JAMES DOBSON

*It is a special gift to be able to view the world
through the eyes of a child.*

God Bless You

Remember you are very special to God as His precious child.
He has promised to complete the good work
He has begun in you. As you continue to grow in Him,
He will teach you to be a blessing to others.

GARY SMALLEY AND JOHN TRENT

I will let God's peace infuse every part of today. As the chaos
swirls and life's demands pull at me on all sides, I will breathe in
God's peace that surpasses all understanding. He has promised
that He would set within me a peace too deeply planted to be
affected by unexpected or exhausting demands.

WENDY MOORE

Lift up your eyes. Your heavenly Father waits to bless you—
in inconceivable ways to make your life what you never
dreamed it could be.

ANNE ORTLUND

A mother is a gift from God
that's blessed in every part...
born through love and loyalty...
conceived within the heart.

I thank God, my mother, for the blessing you are...
for the joy of your laughter...the comfort of your prayers...
the warmth of your smile.

May the LORD, the God of your fathers, increase you a thousand times and bless you as he has promised!

DEUTERONOMY 1:11 NIV

A Reason for Praise

How much of our lives are...well...so daily. How often
our hours are filled with the mundane, seemingly unimportant
things that have to be done, whether at home or work.
These very "daily" tasks could become a celebration of praise.
"It is through consecration," someone has said,
"that drudgery is made divine."

GIGI GRAHAM TCHIVIDJIAN

They that trust the Lord find many things to praise Him for.
Praise follows trust.

LILY MAY GOULD

May your life become one of glad and unending praise
to the Lord as you journey through this world,
and in the world that is to come!

TERESA OF AVILA

Then we, your people, the ones you love and care for,
will thank you over and over and over.
We'll tell everyone we meet how wonderful you are,
how praiseworthy you are!

PSALM 79:13 MSG

Dear Heavenly Father, please go with each member of my
family each day. Protect us as we go our separate ways.
When we meet again, together we will praise and worship You
and give thanks for Your guidance and protection. Amen.

MARILYN JANSEN

*I have never committed the least matter to God,
that I have not had reason for infinite praise.*

Eternal Moments

Friendships, family ties, the companionship of little children,
an autumn forest flung in prodigality against a deep blue sky,
the intricate design and haunting fragrance of a flower...,
the glowing glory of a sunset: the world is aflame
with things of eternal moment.

E. Margaret Clarkson

Life is what we are alive to. It is not length but breadth....
Be alive to...goodness, kindness, purity, love, history, poetry,
music, flowers, stars, God, and eternal hope.

Maltbie D. Babcock

The impetus of God's love comes from within Himself,
to share with us His life and love. It is a beautiful,
eternal gift, held out to us in the hands of love.
All we have to do is say "Yes!"

John Powell

You have made known to me the path of life;
you will fill me with joy in your presence,
with eternal pleasures at your right hand.

Psalm 16:11 niv

When we live life centered around what others like, feel,
and say, we lose touch with our own identity.
I am an eternal being, created by God. I am an
individual with purpose. It's not what I get from life,
but who I am, that makes the difference.

Neva Coyle

All that is not eternal is out of date.

C. S. LEWIS

A Mother's Own Gift

Oh God, You have given me...a life of clay. Put Your big hands
around mine and guide my hands so that every time
I make a mark on this life, it will be Your mark.

GLORIA GAITHER

You know how to give good gifts to your children.
How much more your heavenly Father will give
good things to those who ask him!

MATTHEW 7:11 NCV

Maybe all I could do was mother.... And yet, why did I feel so
fulfilled when I bedded down three kids between clean sheets?
What if raising and instilling values in three children
and turning them into worthwhile human beings would be
the most important contribution I ever made in my lifetime?

ERMA BOMBECK

In the effort to give good and comforting answers to the young
questioners whom we love, we very often arrive at good
and comforting answers for ourselves.

RUTH GOODE

Whatever job I perform—whether changing a diaper,
closing a deal, teaching a class, or writing a book—
when I meet legitimate needs, I am carrying on God's work.

KATHY PEEL

Life, love, and laughter—what priceless gifts to give our children.

PHYLLIS CAMPBELL DRYDEN

What Children Want

Children will not remember you for the material things
you provided, but for the feeling that you cherished them.

GAIL GRENIER SWEET

She is their earth.... She is their food and their bed
and the extra blanket when it grows cold in the night;
she is their warmth and their health and their shelter.

KATHERINE BUTLER HATHAWAY

They might not need me;
but they might.
I'll let my head be just in sight;
A smile as small as mine might be
Precisely their necessity.

EMILY DICKINSON

When children seek attention, affection, encouragement,
and unconditional love, they are not asking for exorbitant gifts.
These are the staples of their soul.

BARBARA FARMER

The very word "motherhood" has an emotional depth
and significance few terms have. It bespeaks nourishment
and safety and sheltering arms.

MARJORIE HOLMES

The everlasting God is your place of safety,
and his arms will hold you up forever.

DEUTERONOMY 33:27 NCV

Loved by God

Blue skies with white clouds on summer days. A myriad of stars
on clear moonlit nights. Tulips and roses and violets
and dandelions and daisies. Bluebirds and laughter
and sunshine and Easter. See how He loves us!

ALICE CHAPIN

We think God's love rises and falls with our performance.
It doesn't.... He loves you for whose you are: you are His child.

MAX LUCADO

God knows everything about us. And He cares about everything.
Moreover, He can manage every situation. And He loves us!
Surely this is enough to open the wellsprings of joy....
And joy is always a source of strength.

HANNAH WHITALL SMITH

This is how much God loved the world: He gave his Son,
his one and only Son. And this is why:
so that no one need be destroyed; by believing in him,
anyone can have a whole and lasting life.

JOHN 3:16 MSG

Our greatness rests solely on the fact that God
in His incomprehensible goodness has bestowed
His love upon us. God does not love us because we are
so valuable; we are valuable because God loves us.

HELMUT THIELICKE

*The Creator thinks enough of you to have sent Someone
very special so that you might have life—abundantly,
joyfully, completely, and victoriously.*

A Mother's Heart

Love grows from our capacity to give what is deepest
within ourselves and also receive what is the deepest within
another person. The heart becomes an ocean strong and deep,
launching all on its tide.

You gave me life and showed me your unfailing love.
My life was preserved by your care.

JOB 10:12 NLT

Being a full-time mother is one of the highest-salaried jobs
in any field since the payment is pure love.

MILDRED B. VERMONT

My mother and I have laughed over nothing and cried
over everything. We understand each other's fears, losses,
and sense of humor. She holds my heart like no one else can.

JANETTE OKE

Women can do no greater thing than to create the climate
of love in their homes. Love which spoils and pampers,
weakens and hampers. Real love strengthens and matures
and leaves the loved one free to grow.

EUGENIA PRICE

A mother's love is the heart of the home.
Her children's sense of security and self-worth are found there.

*No one ever outgrows the need
for a mother's love.*

More to This Life

Life is not intended to be simply a round of work, no matter
how interesting and important that work may be. A moment's
pause to watch the glory of a sunrise or a sunset is soul satisfying,
while a bird's song will set the steps to music all day long.

LAURA INGALLS WILDER

God desires that the work we do bring us enduring joy
and satisfaction. This will naturally happen when our efforts are
labors of love that bring Him glory and praise.

BEVERLY LaHAYE

Get the pattern of your life from God,
then go about your work and be yourself.

PHILLIPS BROOKS

Why is everyone hungry for more?
"More, more," they say. "More, more."
I have God's more-than-enough,
More joy in one ordinary day
Than they get in all their shopping sprees.
At day's end I'm ready for sound sleep,
For you, God, have put my life back together.

PSALM 4:6–8 MSG

If there is a God who speaks anywhere, surely He speaks here:
through waking up and working, through going away
and coming back again, through people you read and books
you meet, through falling asleep in the dark.

FREDERICK BUECHNER

Enjoy the little things. One day you may look back and realize...
they were the big things.

God Hears My Prayer

So wait before the Lord. Wait in the stillness.
And in that stillness, assurance will come to you.
You will know that you are heard; you will know that your Lord
ponders the voice of your humble desires;
you will hear quiet words spoken to you yourself,
perhaps to your grateful surprise and refreshment.

AMY CARMICHAEL

I call on you, O God, for you will answer me;
give ear to me and hear my prayer.
Show the wonder of your great love.

PSALM 17:6–7 NIV

You can talk to God because God listens.
Your voice matters in heaven. He takes you very seriously.
When you enter His presence, the attendants turn to you
to hear your voice. No need to fear that you will be ignored.
Even if you stammer or stumble, even if what you have to say
impresses no one, it impresses God—and He listens.

MAX LUCADO

I prayed to the LORD, and he answered me.
he freed me from all my fears.
Those who look to him for help will be radiant with joy;

PSALM 34:4–5 NLT

*What matters supremely is not the fact that I know God,
but the larger fact which underlies it—the fact that He knows me.*

J. I. PACKER

Everyday Miracles

To be alive, to be able to see, to walk, to have a home, music, paintings, friends—it's all a miracle. I have adopted the technique of living life from miracle to miracle.

ARTUR RUBINSTEIN

I think miracles exist in part as gifts and in part as clues that there is something beyond the flat world we see.

PEGGY NOONAN

The child must know that he is a miracle, that since the beginning of the world there hasn't been, and until the end of the world there will not be, another child like him.

PABLO CASALS

Open my eyes so I can see what you show me of your miracle-wonders.

PSALM 119:18 MSG

The miracles of nature do not seem miracles because they are so common. If no one had ever seen a flower, even a dandelion would be the most startling event in the world.

We couldn't conceive of a miracle if none had ever happened.

LIBBIE FUDIM

When we do the best we can, we never know what miracle is wrought in our life, or in the life of another.

HELEN KELLER

Know that you yourself are a miracle.

Overflowing Grace

Have you ever thought that in every action of grace in your heart
you have the whole omnipotence of God engaged to bless you?

ANDREW MURRAY

In difficulties, I can drink freely of God's power
and experience His touch of refreshment and blessing—
much like an invigorating early spring rain.

ANABEL GILLHAM

You can be sure that God will take care of everything you need,
his generosity exceeding even yours in the glory that
pours from Jesus. Our God and Father abounds in glory
that just pours out into eternity.

PHILIPPIANS 4:18 MSG

I'll never be a millionaire but I have something
better than that. I have my children, good friends,
a place to call home, and wonderful relatives.
These are so many of life's wonderful blessings!

All perfect gifts are from above
and all our blessings show
The amplitude of God's dear love
which any heart may know.

LAURA LEE RANDALL

*From his abundance we have all received
one gracious blessing after another.*

JOHN 1:16 NLT

Encouraging Words

Encouragement is being a good listener, being positive,
letting others know you accept them for who they are.
It is offering hope, caring about
the feelings of another, understanding.

GIGI GRAHAM TCHIVIDJIAN

A mother is one who knows you as you really are,
understands where you've been, accepts who you've become,
and still gently invites you to grow.

A word of encouragement to those we meet, a cheerful smile
in the supermarket, a card or letter to a friend, a readiness to
witness when opportunity is given—all are practical ways
in which we may let His light shine through us.

ELIZABETH B. JONES

Be joyful. Grow to maturity. Encourage each other.
Live in harmony and peace. Then the God
of love and peace will be with you.

2 CORINTHIANS 13:11 NLT

Some days, it is enough encouragement just to watch the clouds
break up and disappear, leaving behind a blue patch of sky
and bright sunshine that is so warm upon my face.
It's a glimpse of divinity; a kiss from heaven.

There are times when encouragement means such a lot.
And a word is enough to convey it.

GRACE STRICKER DAWSON

Joys of Motherhood

Sense of humor; God's great gift
causes spirits to uplift,
Helps to make our bodies mend;
lightens burdens; cheers a friend;
Tickles children; elders grin
at this warmth that glows within;
Surely in the great hereafter
heaven must be full of laughter!

Truth...has got to be concrete. And there's nothing more
concrete than dealing with babies, burps, bottles and frogs.

JEANE KIRKPATRICK

Now, as always, the most automated
appliance in a household is the mother.

BEVERLY JONES

When children's eyes are smiling
'Tis God's love that's shining through
With glints of joy and laughter
What good medicine for you!

MARGARET FISHBACK POWERS

A good day: When the wheels of your shopping cart
all go in the same direction.

*A cheerful look brings joy to the heart;
good news makes for good health.*

PROVERBS 15:30 NLT

Special Gifts We Share

We should make the most of what God gives,
both the bounty and the capacity to enjoy it,
accepting what's given and delighting in the work.
It's God's gift! God deals out joy in the present, the now.

ECCLESIASTES 5:18 MSG

God's designs regarding you, and His methods
of bringing about these designs, are infinitely wise.

MADAME JEANNE GUYON

Our greatest responsibility today may be
the unselfish sacrifice of our time, talent, and love
in the lives of those little ones around us.

SUSAN DOWNS

Give, and it will be given to you. A good measure,
pressed down, shaken together and running over,
will be poured into your lap. For with the measure you use,
it will be measured to you.

LUKE 6:38 NIV

Each one of us is God's special work of art. Through us,
He teaches and inspires, delights and encourages,
informs and uplifts all those who view our lives.

JONI EARECKSON TADA

God gave me my gifts. I will do all I can
to show Him how grateful I am to Him.

GRACE LIVINGSTON HILL

God Loves Our Children

For my dear little child I'd lasso the moon
and give you my love on a silver spoon.
I'd run 'round the world and back again, too,
to grant you the hope of days bright and new.
But all that I have and all that I do
is nothing compared to God's love for you.

Children of the heavenly Father
Safely in His bosom gather;
Nestling bird nor star in heaven
Such a refuge e'er was given.

CAROLINA SANDELL BERG

How great is the love the Father has lavished on us,
that we should be called children of God!
And that is what we are!

1 JOHN 3:1 NIV

God is so big He can cover the whole world with His love,
and so small He can curl up inside your heart.

JUNE MASTERS BACHER

If nothing seems to go my way today, this is my happiness:
God is my Father and I am His child.

BASILEA SCHLINK

*After the love of God, a mother's affection
is the greatest treasure here below.*

The Richness of Friendship

We are so very rich if we know just a few people
in a way in which we know no others.

CATHERINE BRAMWELL-BOOTH

Knowing what to say is not always necessary;
just the presence of a caring friend
can make a world of difference.

SHERI CURRY

If we would build on a sure foundation in friendship,
we must love friends for their sake rather than for our own.

CHARLOTTE BRONTË

A friend hears the song in my heart
and sings it to me when my memory fails.

Stay true to the Lord. I love you and long to see you,
dear friends, for you are my joy.

PHILIPPIANS 4:1 NLT

I am only as strong as the coffee I drink,
the hairspray I use, and the friends I have.

A friend understands what you are trying to say...
even when your thoughts aren't fitting into words.

ANN D. PARRISH

Insomuch as any one pushes you nearer to God,
he or she is your friend.

FRENCH PROVERB

Live, Laugh, Love

Whole-hearted, ready laughter heals, encourages,
relaxes anyone within hearing distance. The laughter that
springs from love makes wide the space around—
gives room for the loved one to enter in.

EUGENIA PRICE

People can be divided into three groups: Those who
make things happen, those who watch things happen,
and those who wonder what happened.

Today's Forecast: Partly rational with brief periods
of coherent thought giving way to complete apathy by tonight.

SHERRIE WEAVER

If you can learn to laugh in spite of the circumstances
that surround you, you will enrich others, enrich yourself,
and more than that, you will last!

BARBARA JOHNSON

The best laughter, the laughter that can heal,
the laughter that has the truest ring, is the laughter
that flowers out of a love for life and its Giver.

MAXINE HANCOCK

Let all those who seek You
rejoice and be glad in You.

PSALM 40:16 NKJV

*A good laugh is as good
as a prayer sometimes.*

LUCY MAUD MONTGOMERY

I Believe

Faith allows us to continually delight in life
since we have placed our needs in God's hands.

JANET L. SMITH

I believe in the sun even if it isn't shining.
I believe in love even when I am alone.
I believe in God even when He is silent.

Let your roots grow down into him, and let your lives
be built on him. Then your faith will grow strong in the truth
you were taught, and you will overflow with thankfulness.

COLOSSIANS 2:7 NLT

Faith is not an effort, a striving, a ceaseless seeking,
as so many earnest souls suppose, but rather a letting go,
an abandonment, an abiding rest in God that nothing,
not even the soul's shortcomings, can disturb.

Be alert. Continue strong in the faith.
Have courage, and be strong.

1 CORINTHIANS 16:13 NCV

I do not seek to understand that I may believe,
but I believe in order to understand. For this I believe—
that unless I believe, I should not understand.

ANSELM OF CANTERBURY

*Within each of us there is an inner place
where the living God Himself longs to dwell,
our sacred center of belief.*

A Heart Full of Joy

Our hearts were made for joy. Our hearts were made
to enjoy the One who created them. Too deeply planted
to be much affected by the ups and downs of life,
this joy is a knowing and a being known by our Creator.
He sets our hearts alight with radiant joy.

WENDY MOORE

When hands reach out in friendship,
hearts are touched with joy.

If one is joyful, it means that one is faithfully living for God,
and that nothing else counts; and if one gives joy to others one is
doing God's work. With joy without and joy within, all is well.

JANET ERSKINE STUART

All who seek the LORD will praise him.
Their hearts will rejoice with everlasting joy.

PSALM 22:26 NLT

As we grow in our capacities to see and enjoy the joys
that God has placed in our lives, life becomes a glorious
experience of discovering His endless wonders.

Since you get more joy out of giving joy to others,
you should put a good deal of thought into the happiness
that you are able to give.

ELEANOR ROOSEVELT

*Joy is warm and radiant and clamors
for expressions and experience.*

DOROTHY SEGOVIA

Mother and Child

There is no other closeness in human life like the closeness
between a mother and her baby—chronologically, physically,
and spiritually they are just a few heartbeats away
from being the same person.

SUSAN CHEVER

No joy in nature is so sublimely affecting as the joy
of a mother at the good fortune of her child.

JEAN PAUL RICHTER

She is clothed with strength and dignity,
and she laughs without fear of the future.
When she speaks, her words are wise,
and she gives instructions with kindness.
She carefully watches everything in her
household and suffers nothing from laziness.
Her children stand and bless her.

PROVERBS 31:25–28 NLT

All mothers are rich when they love their children....
Their love is always the most beautiful of joys.

MAURICE MAETERLINCK

There is an enduring tenderness in the love of a mother to a
[child] that transcends all other affections of the heart.

WASHINGTON IRVING

*A mother's arms are made of tenderness
and children sleep soundly in them.*

VICTOR HUGO

A Gift to Cherish

Everything in life is most fundamentally a gift.
And you receive it best, and you live it best,
by holding it with very open hands.

LEO O'DONOVAN

How beautiful it is to be alive!
To wake each morn as if the Maker's grace
Did us afresh from nothingness derive,
That we might sing "How happy is our case!
How beautiful it is to be alive."

HENRY SEPTIMUS SUTTON

Every day we live is a priceless gift of God, loaded with
possibilities to learn something new, to gain fresh insights.

DALE EVANS ROGERS

Into all our lives, in many simple, familiar, homely ways,
God infuses this element of joy from the surprises of life,
which unexpectedly brighten our days,
and fill our eyes with light.

SAMUEL LONGFELLOW

Your life is a gift from God,
And it is a privilege to share it.
Today and always,
Know that you have a
very special place in others' hearts—
And in His.

God's gift has restored our relationship with him and given us back our lives. And there's more life to come—an eternity of life!

TITUS 3:7 MSG

Be Encouraged

God, bless all young mothers at end of day.
Kneeling wearily with each small one to hear them pray.
Too tired to rise when done...and yet they do;
longing just to sleep one whole night through.
Too tired to sleep.... Too tired to pray....
God, bless all young mothers at close of day.

RUTH BELL GRAHAM

I'm sure now I'll see God's goodness in the
exuberant earth. Stay with GOD!
Take heart. Don't quit.

PSALM 27:13 MSG

Being taken for granted can be a compliment.
It means that you've become a comfortable,
trusted person in another person's life.

JOYCE BROTHERS

Calm me, O Lord, as You stilled the storm,
Still me, O Lord, keep me from harm.
Let all the tumult within me cease,
Enfold me, Lord, in Your peace.

CELTIC TRADITIONAL

Faith is the bucket of power lowered by the
rope of prayer into the well of God's abundance.
What we bring up depends upon what we let down.
We have every encouragement to use a big bucket.

VIRGINIA WHITMAN

*The Scriptures give us hope and encouragement as we
wait patiently for God's promises to be fulfilled.*

ROMANS 15:4 NLT

God's Promises for a Mother's Heart
A Promise Journal

© 2010 Ellie Claire™ Gift and Paper Corp.
Minneapolis 55438
www.ellieclaire.com

ISBN 978-1-60936-129-7

Excluding Scripture verses and deity pronouns, in some quotations references to men and
masculine pronouns have been replaced with gender-neutral or feminine references.
Additionally, in some quotations we have carefully updated verb forms
and wordings that may distract modern readers.

Compiled by Barbara Farmer
Cover and interior designed by Lisa and Jeff Franke

Printed in China.